Helmsley Castle

John R Kenyon

CONTENTS

Tour of Helmsley Castle

OVERVIEW AND SETTING

Helmsley Castle stands on an outcrop of rock in the valley of the river Rye, overlooking the historic market town to the east. The central platform of the castle is surrounded by inner and outer ditches, with a rampart between the two. Even allowing for the fact that the profile of the dry ditches is the result of work undertaken after Helmsley was taken into State care in 1923, its earthworks, which would have required an enormous feat of engineering, are among the most substantial of any castle in the country. Helmsley was founded in the early 12th century by Walter Espec, but most of the surviving masonry dates from about 1200 onwards, the work of various members of the de Ros family up to the middle of the 14th century. The castle consists of an outer bailey, now devoid of features, and an inner bailey, the core of the castle, which was originally divided in two by a 12th-century wall and possibly a ditch. This division probably ran north-east to south-west between the later east and west towers. To the north of the medieval castle lay an orchard and gardens, while to the west were two parks on the site of the present Duncombe Park.

In the 1570s and 1580s the Manners family built a mansion inside the castle, part of which remains on the west side of the inner bailey. The rest of the castle buildings and defences were dismantled following the Civil War and are now ruinous. Both the castle and the ruins of Rievaulx Abbey, which stand about three miles to the north-west, were incorporated in the 18th century into the designed landscape of Duncombe Park.

Facing page: The east tower from the west, with the remains of the north gate in the foreground

Above: Fragment from Helmsley Castle of a 13th-century green glazed pot decorated with a face
Below: Helmsley Castle and the surrounding area

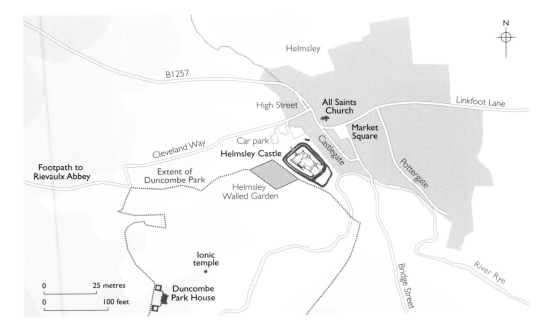

Above: The south barbican gatehouse: its central section between the two rounded towers was remodelled in the 16th century

Below: The decorated stonework of the gatehouse passage may have been salvaged from Rievaulx Abbey

■ SOUTH BARBICAN

The south barbican is approached across the medieval outer bailey. This would have had earth and timber defences, although an early 20th-century plan shows a section of a later wall in the north-west corner, and traces of structures were revealed during geophysical survey work in 1995. Service buildings, such as a stable, may have stood in the outer bailey, and there was probably a gateway. The shape of the bailey was altered in the 18th century to create an entrance to Duncombe Park.

The south barbican consists of a central twin-towered gatehouse, originally approached across a drawbridge, flanked by curtain walls with rounded towers at either end. All four towers had one or two floors. The barbican was built between 1227 and 1285. The gatehouse passage had a portcullis with a double-leaf wooden door behind. Some arrow slits remain – others were later widened into windows. A series of rectangular sockets at the tops of the walls held timber beams for a projecting wooden gallery or hourd, which allowed defenders to cover the approaches to the walls. At either end of the barbican, doorways opened onto the ramparts. The entrance to the western tower may have had its own drawbridge, as there is evidence for a small drawbridge pit in front of the doorway.

In the 1570s the exterior of the gatehouse and its entrance passage were rebuilt. The carved masonry of the passage might be medieval material reused from Rievaulx Abbey. A carving of an imp on the right-hand side was perhaps placed there to ward off evil spirits. The sockets above the passage entrance

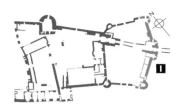

may have been part of the drawbridge arrangement or were holes through which pistols could be fired from the floor above. Graffiti carved by visitors from the 17th century onwards can be seen on either side of the entrance.

Originally the barbican towers were open at the back, but they were enclosed when the castle underwent major refurbishment during the late 13th to early 14th centuries. Two chambers were built against the inner face of the west curtain, the larger of the two being provided with a fireplace and a latrine. A latrine turret was also added on the east side of the gatehouse. The remains of a fireplace and a drain in the west tower of the gatehouse suggest that there could have been a small kitchen here. This well-appointed accommodation – heated chambers served by a private kitchen and indoor latrines – may have been built for the constable of the castle. Castle gates often provided accommodation for the constable, who was often an important local man in charge of his lord's affairs as well as the day-to-day running and security of the building. In 1343 records show that Helmsley's constable was paid the meagre sum of 3d. per day and was entitled to a robe worth 20s. annually.

These defences were not dismantled following the Civil War siege of Helmsley in 1644, and were probably retained to form an impressive approach to the Elizabethan mansion within the inner bailey.

A Troublesome Prisoner

A curious story concerning an early 14th-century constable of Helmsley, William Starre, demonstrates how a constable could be asked to carry out important duties on behalf of the lord or even the king. In October 1338 King Edward III (r.1327–77) wrote to William de Ros III, who owned Helmsley Castle from 1316, stating that a woman, Joan Fletcher, had been excommunicated for 'contumacy', wilful disobedience regarding the authority of the Archbishop of York, William Melton. She was placed in the custody of Thomas Overton, one of the Sheriff of York's men. On the discovery of a plot to kill Thomas and free Joan, Overton took refuge in Helmsley Castle, placing Joan in the keeping of William Starre, 'until Holy Church is satisfied or until her release is ordered by the king.' We do not know the precise details of the offence, nor of Joan's subsequent fate.

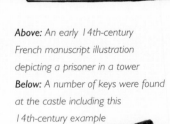

Above: An early 14th-century French manuscript illustration depicting a prisoner in a tower

Below: A number of keys were found at the castle including this 14th-century example

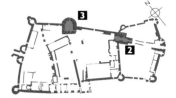

🄱 SOUTH GATE

A pair of 'wing walls' links the defences of the inner bailey to the south barbican. These were built in about 1300 to provide additional protection for the south gate. Arches in the walls at ditch level are likely to have been small doorways to allow access to the ditch. The footings of a rounded tower on the wing wall can be seen just to the right of the south gate.

This gate was built in about 1200 and formed the main entrance into the inner bailey. It was a rectangular tower with a first-floor chamber, and possibly another floor above that, the wide passage beneath being protected by a portcullis and inward-opening doors, the pivots for which are visible on one side. A drawbridge pit was added in the 13th century when the south barbican was first built. It comprises an inner and outer abutment on either side of the ditch, originally spanned by a drawbridge where the modern bridge now sits. The inner abutment, containing an open pit that would have been covered by the drawbridge when lowered, has three doorways or posterns in the basement to provide access to the ditches. A staircase on the west side led down to the base of the pit, and up to the crest, or berm, of the bank. These posterns acted as 'back doors' to enable the garrison to sally out to harass attackers without opening the main gates, and to provide access for labourers to maintain the banks and ditches. A small chamber on the east side of the gate allowed a porter to keep watch over the east wing wall and the approach to the gate.

Beyond the passage, a length of masonry abuts the original curtain wall. These footings are the remains of a porch and steps that provided access to the wall-walk. At the far side of the stairs there is a postern in the curtain wall, now blocked.

Above: View south-west towards the wing wall spanning the inner ditch
Below: The south gate formed the main entrance into the inner bailey
🄰 Remains of south gate
🄱 Inner drawbridge abutment
🄲 Outer drawbridge abutment
🄳 Location of drawbridge
🄴 Posterns

Left: The remains of the east tower from the north-east. The sloping scars of the original roofline of the 13th-century tower are clearly visible. The rubble from the collapsed north-east face of the tower can be seen in the foreground
Below: Elevation showing the two main phases of construction of the east tower. Built originally by about 1200, the tower was heightened and the turrets added in the 14th century

3 EAST TOWER

Despite its ruined condition, the east tower remains a dominant feature of the castle today. When first built by Robert de Ros II (d.1226/7), about the year 1200, the tower consisted of a vaulted basement with a central pillar, and an upper floor containing the main chamber. The tower would have been visible for miles around, a symbol of the power of the lords of Helmsley.

A staircase within the wall in the west corner of the tower gave access to the basement, and a postern opened onto the rampart. The basement was lit by two narrow windows in the south-west wall, although there may have been further windows in the destroyed outer face. It is likely to have been used for storage. The original upper floor was a grand chamber, lit by three lancet windows, with a fourth above, just below the line of the original roof; again, there would also have been windows or loops in the missing north-east face of the tower. Footings for steps that led to the wall-walk and to an entrance into the first floor can be seen on the south-east side of the building. There was also a first-floor doorway on the north-west side of the

East Tower Elevation

	Late 14th century
	1285–1342
	1190–1200

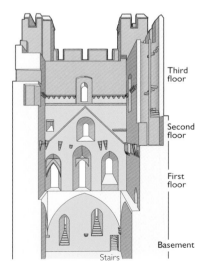

Third floor

Second floor

First floor

Basement

Stairs

tower, later blocked. This first-floor room may originally have been used for conducting formal and judicial business.

In the 14th century William de Ros II (d.1316) raised the tower to create additional stately rooms, giving the tower its present appearance. This heightening, coupled with the insertion of a vault in the original first floor that partly obscured the lancets, gave the tower two additional storeys, the uppermost being an attic with a wooden floor. The staircase was extended upwards for access. A doorway, through which the basement is entered today, was inserted in the south corner of the tower and was originally set within a porch. The heightened tower has 'ear' turrets (small turrets in pairs), comparable to those seen on earlier royal buildings such as the Beauchamp Tower, built in 1281 to overawe visitors approaching the main entrance to the Tower of London. The tower at Helmsley would have been used to the same effect; to impress visitors approaching the castle from the town, the centre of which was being re-planned at this time, and from further afield. The turret to the west had a lead roof, which may have been reached by a ladder, while the other turret was flagged in stone, with a stone stair allowing access for a sentry. The parapet walk was paved. The fine rooms within the tower may have been used by King Edward III when he visited Helmsley in 1334.

Later Alterations

A final alteration came in the late 14th century when a fire damaged the tower, and the uppermost floor was replaced by a stone vault. At the same time a latrine was inserted in the south-east wall, projecting from the tower. Other minor changes included the blocking of a second-floor window on the north-west side to create a fireplace. Following the surrender of the castle during the Civl War in 1644, the outer face of the tower was undermined and brought down with gunpowder to prevent reuse. The rubble is visible in the inner ditch.

Above: Projecting turrets on the late 13th-century Beauchamp Tower at the Tower of London: those on Helmsley's east tower create a similar effect
Left: This 18th-century view of the east tower in the snow by Thomas Girtin (1775–1802) shows the ruins already substantially overgrown

Facing page: The east tower from the west. The change in the masonry towards the top of the tower shows where it was heightened in the 14th century

Above: View south-east across
the inner bailey
A Chapel
B Well
C Kitchen
D Pantry
E Buttery
F Hall

Below: A mid 14th-century Flemish
illustration of a priest celebrating Mass.
In 1343 Helmsley's chaplain was
being paid to say Mass daily for the
souls of the past lords of Helmsley
Below right: One of the green glazed
roof tiles **1** and fragments of
decorated window glass **2** which
may have come from the chapel

4 CHAPEL

The chapel, consecrated in 1246, must have replaced an earlier
building from the time of Walter Espec, although it is not
known where the original chapel was situated.

In order to accommodate a strict east-to-west alignment,
the rectangular building appears to sit awkwardly across the
courtyard, with its north-east corner almost abutting the east
tower. At the east end of the chapel there were doorways in
the north and south walls, and there was a third doorway at
the south-west corner. The chapel may have contained a
gallery or closet at the west end from which the de Ros family
would have observed the Mass, while members of their
household stood in the nave below. Mosaic floor tiles similar
to those at Rievaulx Abbey, as well as fragments of window
glass and green glazed roof tiles found in the inner bailey, may
have come from the chapel. The chapel was served by a
chaplain. In 1343 he was being paid a stipend of five marks
annually (one mark was 13s. 4d.).

In the 16th century the chapel appears to have been used
as a kitchen, with a fireplace inserted at the east end where
the altar would have been, and the west end subdivided. It is
not known where the Tudor chapel which replaced this one
was located.

5 WELL

Beyond the chapel lies a low, arched structure that covers the medieval well, the original depth of which is uncertain. This appears to have been the only source of water in the castle, conveniently positioned near to the kitchen range.

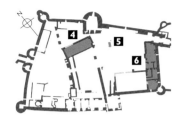

6 KITCHEN RANGE

The kitchen and associated rooms lay between the south gate and the south-west tower, against the curtain wall of about 1200. The remains that can be seen today date from the late 13th and early 14th centuries, and presumably replaced an earlier domestic range on this site.

The large room at the north-eastern end was the kitchen. Here, there is a fireplace in the north-west wall, while against the south gate is a pair of pastry ovens. These were more common from the 16th century and so are likely to be later additions. The setting for a medieval or later boiler in which meat and fish would be cooked in a cauldron can be seen next to the ovens.

South of the kitchen was an open yard, later subdivided. To the south of this yard were the pantry, where bread and tableware were stored, and the buttery beyond, from where drinks were dispensed. Both the pantry and the buttery had doorways that opened into the hall. The pantry appears to have been subdivided soon after construction, with the creation of a room in the south-eastern half adjacent to the curtain wall. This room had a grilled window, from where a household servant could have checked the quality and quantity of the food prepared in the kitchen. This official would also have marshalled the staff before they processed into the great hall to serve the food and drink.

Below: A locally made (Ryedale ware) 16th-century pot used for cooking, found at Helmsley Castle
Bottom: View south-west along the kitchen range. A senior household servant may have sat in the room beyond this window, inspecting food before it was taken into the great hall

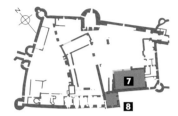

Ale and wine were stored in the cool vaulted basement of the south-west tower and brought up to the buttery to be served. The structure in one corner may have been a brewing furnace for ale, and was possibly added at a slightly late date; beer did not become popular until the 15th century.

The kitchen range would only have operated fully when the lord of the castle was present. When the de Ros family was absent, with only the constable and assistants in residence, a small kitchen for staff in the gatehouse of the south barbican may have been used instead.

7 HALL

The main hall dates from the decades either side of 1300, presumably replacing an earlier hall built on this site in about 1200. The hall was where the household dined every day and grand feasts were held, and where the castle's estates were administered, with hearings and lawsuits.

The width of the room, coupled with the remains of the buttresses against one wall, suggest that the building was aisled, with columns giving support to a pitched roof. Water from the roof was channelled into a drain just to the south of the west tower, the water being used to flush a latrine.

A wooden screens passage at the south-east end divided the hall from the service range. This passage could be accessed from the service range as well as by guests from the courtyard. The family and the most important guests would have entered the hall from the west tower, through a doorway in the corner. The lord and his closest relations and chief guests would have eaten at a table set upon a dais against the wall by this west door. Those on the dais would have been served first, and then others who sat in order of rank below the dais. The hall probably continued to be used on formal occasions into Tudor times.

There is no evidence for a fireplace, so the room must have been heated by a central hearth, with a louvre in the roof to allow smoke to escape – a design not unusual, even in the later Middle Ages.

Above: Various objects associated with dining have been found here: people carried small daggers such as this one (top) to use at table throughout the Middle Ages; this fragment (below) is the upper part of a late medieval glazed cistern or bung-hole jar. Liquids, such as ale, would have been served via a tap at the base
Below: A late 15th-century illustration of servants decanting wine from large barrels and a jug, for serving at table

Left: The basement of the west tower. In the ceiling can be seen the impression of hazel wicker shuttering, the frame used to support the plaster for the ceiling between the vault ribs

West Tower Floor Plans

1122–53	14th century
1190–1200	16th century

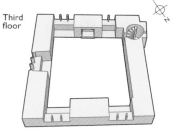

Third floor

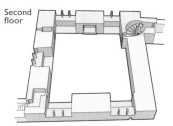

Second floor

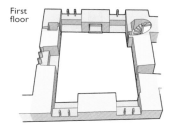

First floor

Ground floor

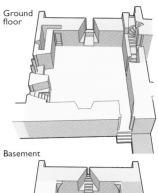

Basement

8 WEST TOWER

The tower, built originally by Robert de Ros II in about 1200, was used throughout its existence as a solar – a private great chamber that provided intimate accommodation for the castle's owners, away from the adjacent chamber block on its north-western side. It is one of the finest examples of a solar tower in the country. It sat partly over the 12th-century wall that had divided the inner bailey of Walter Espec's castle in two.

When first built, it comprised a basement with two floors above, providing views over the extensive parkland to the west and south. The rooms were probably subdivided into at least two chambers per floor. In the early 14th century the tower was heightened, another floor being added, and the south-west wall was rebuilt closer to the inner ditch. A latrine was inserted on each floor in the southern corner. A doorway in the west corner led onto the curtain wall at second-floor level. The third floor was added in the 16th century, and at the same time new windows and fireplaces were inserted, the fireplaces blocking the 14th-century windows in the south-west wall.

Basement

Steps lead down to the basement, which was used for storage and has a window in the north-east and south-west walls. The window overlooking the ditch has seats, and there are peacocks, the de Ros emblem, carved at either end of the window arch. These date from when the castle was enlarged in the decades either side of 1300. This impressive window suggests that an accounting officer might have worked here, taking advantage of the natural daylight when auditing goods as they came and went.

Parks and Landscape

The landscape around the medieval castle would have been dominated by farmland, both pasture and arable, as well as woodland and enclosed parkland.

Great landowners created parks for recreation such as hunting, and many castles had gardens adjacent to them, or even within their walls.

At Helmsley, the 'Old Park' lay to the south-east and 'Le Haye', a small inner park close to the west side of the castle, existed from at least the middle of the 13th century, being mentioned in a document of 1250–51. The 'New Park', an enlargement of Le Haye to the west of the castle, is mentioned from 1302. These private parks were enclosed with pales or banks, and traces of the earthwork that surrounded Le Haye are visible in Duncombe Park. Medieval 'ortyerdes' (orchards) and a garden ('rapark') lay to the north, where the car park is today.

The de Ros family employed a parker to oversee the care of the parks – in the mid 14th century a parker named William de Middleton was paid 1½d. per day and provided with a new robe each year as a reflection of

his status. A maker of paling is also recorded – he received 3s. per year and a quarter (about 13kg) of corn and rye every 12 weeks and was presumably employed to maintain the park boundaries. On a number of occasions from the late 13th century, however, the de Ros family complained of people breaking into their parks at Helmsley and elsewhere, hunting deer. On one occasion in 1370, trees were felled, deer taken, and de Ros servants attacked and injured at Harswell in the East Riding.

In the 18th century, the castle ruins formed a backdrop to the designed landscape of Duncombe Park. An 'Ionic temple' in the form of a rotunda, from where the castle could be viewed, was built on the garden terrace to the east of Duncombe Park in about 1730. The walled garden below the castle was established in 1758 to supply produce for Duncombe Park, and was rescued from dereliction in the 1990s.

Above: A late 14th-century scene of a deer hunt
Below: Plan of the medieval parks around Helmsley Castle, in relation to the later parkland of Duncombe Park

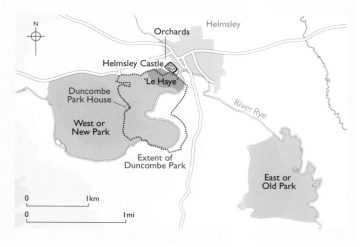

Interior

The ground floor is entered through the original round-headed doorway. The door in the north-western wall led to the staircase to the upper floors and to the west range; there is an original fireplace with an oven in the north-east wall, with further fireplaces above, while the south-west and south-east walls contain 14th-century windows. Doorways in the south corner of the ground, first and second floors led to latrines.

The floor levels were rearranged in the 16th century and the remains of wooden joists for the Elizabethan flooring are visible inside the tower. A 'great chamber' mentioned in the 1636 inventory of the castle, an intimate room for family and the most important guests, might have been located in an upper floor of the west tower. The 16th-century fireplaces on the upper floors originally had carved roses and shields in the spandrels, but most have been weathered away.

Above: A late 12th-century fireplace with an oven in the north-east wall of the west tower
Below: Interior of the west tower looking south. The fireplaces seen here were added in the 16th century, blocking earlier 14th-century windows

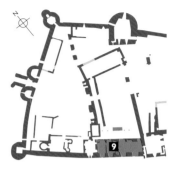

Right: The west range of the castle comprises the west tower, the central chamber block and the latrine tower. These buildings formed the core of the Elizabethan manor house

A West tower
B Original doorway of about 1200
C Doorway from first floor onto loggia balcony
D Base of medieval chimney
E Footings of steps that led onto the loggia balcony
F Chamber block
G Footings of Elizabethan long gallery
H Latrine tower

Below: The middle chamber on the ground floor of the chamber block with its Tudor fireplace and window

9 CHAMBER BLOCK AND ELIZABETHAN RANGE

At the same time as the west tower was being built in about 1200, a chamber block was raised next to it. Intriguingly, remains of early 12th-century masonry, presumably from an earlier building, can be seen in the outer wall. The chamber block provided the main accommodation for the castle's residents, and probably consisted of a ground floor, or undercroft, with a single large room on the upper floor, open to the roof. This building was transformed from the 1570s into part of an Elizabethan mansion.

Exterior

At the south-eastern end of the chamber block, to the right of the present doorway, is a blocked round-headed doorway that led into the medieval undercroft. To the right of this is the base of a medieval chimney, and further along the wall, by the entrance into the ground floor at the north-west end, can be seen the remains of a medieval window and door jamb.

In the 1570s a loggia, or covered walkway, ran along the length of this range. The stone bases for the timber columns of this loggia remain in position; two are incorporated

into walling that formed the base of steps that led to a balcony that ran along the top of the loggia.

Ground Floor

The ground floor was originally an undercroft below the medieval great chamber. It was perhaps used as storage and for other domestic facilities such as servant accommodation, and may have been divided into separate rooms. The ground floor was adapted in Tudor times and consists of three rooms. The room nearest to the west tower has a large 16th-century fireplace, and three four-light windows and, in Tudor times, was possibly the servants' dining room or a small, private kitchen for the lord. Access to the west tower staircase was pushed through the masonry of the south-east wall in the 16th century; the remains of the original medieval doorway into the tower lie beyond. An inventory of the castle from 1636 mentions that this room had two long tables, a cupboard, four 'forms' or benches, and an 'alms tub' – a container for the storage of leftover food for distribution to the poor.

A panelled partition divided this room from the small middle chamber, furnished with a Tudor fireplace and lit by Elizabethan windows. The main feature is the medieval

Below: According to a 17th-century inventory, an 'alms tub' or dole cupboard, which may have looked like this one from Haddon Hall, Derbyshire, stood in the ground floor of the chamber block. It was used to store food to give to the poor

Right: Detail of a Tudor feast with musicians and dancing from a portrait of Sir Henry Unton of about 1596. The dining room on the upper floor of the chamber block at Helmsley was probably used for similarly grand dining and entertainments

Below: A 16th- to 17th-century chamber pot from Helmsley

Bottom: The north-western chamber on the upper floor still contains some 16th-century plasterwork. The design includes mermaids, dolphins and heraldry

staircase leading down to a small door that originally opened onto a bridge across the inner ditch; the steps would have continued up to the first floor. The north-western room also has Elizabethan windows and both small chambers may have housed important servants.

Upper Floor

Originally built as one single chamber in the 13th century, the first floor now comprises two fine, well-lit rooms. In early Tudor times, however, the north-western chamber was divided into two small rooms, each with a fireplace. The round-headed doorway that led to the medieval latrine tower was blocked in the 16th century, when the new door was inserted. The first room, nearest to the latrine tower, may have been for the lord or lady's personal servants, with a bedchamber or withdrawing chamber beyond. An oriel window in this bedchamber overlooked the park to the west and there are remnants of decorative plasterwork on the ceiling and running along the top of the walls, with the Manners family's coat of arms. This was possibly the room

described as 'My lord's bed chamber' in a 1636 inventory of
the castle. The heraldry was probably painted in bright colours,
but the ceilings in this range may always have been white. The
plasterwork also includes decorative dolphins and mermaids,
symbols frequently used to signify diligence and eloquence
respectively.

To the south-east is a large room, probably the private
dining room of the 16th-century mansion, entered through a
door set in a handsome carved Elizabethan wooden partition.
The chamber is also well lit, with an oriel window and three
eight-light windows. The fireplace in the north-east wall is
dated 1582 and is decorated with polygonal panels with knots
and roses. The decorative plasterwork is more extensive here
than in the bedchamber. The impressive fireplace, the heraldic
frieze and the fine ceiling emphasize the high status of this
room in the late 16th century. The south-eastern wall has a
door to the west tower, as well as a blocked medieval
doorway that originally led to the west tower. The doorway
that leads outside onto the modern wooden stair may
originally have led onto the balcony that ran above the
Elizabethan loggia, leading to a long gallery.

Above: Detail from the finely
carved wooden partition between
the two upper-floor rooms of the
chamber block
Below: The dining room contains fine
wood panelling, a decorated fireplace
dated 1582, and plasterwork on the
ceiling and walls

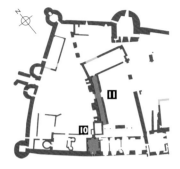

10 LATRINE TOWER

This tower, ruinous by the early 20th century, is complicated to understand as a result of much rebuilding. The tower contained latrines for the domestic range from about 1300 when it was built against the north-west end of the chamber block and the inner face of the curtain wall; the two latrines were originally divided by a wooden partition and lit by small windows. The adjacent small rectangular opening in the north-west wall was a drain for waste water. Above the latrines can be seen the remains of the medieval wall-walk, with a 16th-century window above. Recesses next to the latrines may have been used to keep a candle and possibly also cleansing materials, such as moss. The quality of the 14th-century masonry indicates that the latrines were originally for the use of the de Ros family.

The north-west wall has two fireplaces in the upper floor, which was added in the late 16th or 17th century to provide additional accommodation for servants. These upper-floor rooms are probably those referred to in the 1636 inventory as 'Thre rooms up the backe stayres'. Below these fireplaces is a blocked window and a fireplace, added in the 16th century. The southern wall contains the passage that connected the latrine tower with the chamber beyond, and also bears the scar of an external staircase that may have led to the wall-walk in about 1200, but which was later incorporated into the latrine tower.

Right: The shafts for the two latrines in the latrine tower. The quality of the ashlar, or dressed stonework, is a notable feature here

⑪ GALLERY

An important feature of numerous great Tudor and Jacobean houses was a long gallery, with decorative ceilings and panelling, and often hung with family portraits. This was a room for exercise and general conversations, perhaps even dancing. A long gallery range was built at Helmsley from the 1570s. It ran across the inner bailey between the chamber block and the medieval chapel. Only the footings of this range can be seen today. It was a timber-framed building set on stone foundations – an unusual arrangement. Where long galleries were added to other castles they were usually of masonry, as at Berry Pomeroy, Devon, and Raglan in Monmouthshire. The gallery would have been at first-floor level, and the ground floor was enclosed, with a passage connecting the north and south sides of the inner bailey. There may have been a small private garden, sandwiched between the gallery and the remains of the 12th-century wall that originally divided the inner bailey in two. The gallery was heated with fireplaces and had latrines housed in small closets. The bases of these can be seen in the masonry footings.

Beyond the chapel, between the east and north-east towers, were further 16th-century lodgings. The purpose of the rectangular building whose walls lie outside the latrine tower is unknown, although it is assumed that it dates from the 14th century as the long gallery's footings abut it.

Top: View south along the footings of the long gallery towards the chamber block. The gallery itself was at first-floor level, with rooms below probably used for storage
Above: The long gallery at Helmsley may have looked similar to this gallery at Haddon Hall, remodelled by John Manners, second son of the 1st Earl of Rutland, in the late 16th century

12 BREWHOUSE AND 13 BAKEHOUSE

In the north-west corner of the castle are the remains of the brewhouse and bakehouse. They were probably built either in the 15th century, when beer brewing became more common, or in the 16th century, before the west range of the castle was converted into the Tudor mansion. This was perhaps the only area of the inner bailey where there was room for these new buildings.

The bakehouse stood at the north-western end. Its large bread oven was altered to accommodate a small boiling furnace with edge-on slates, where water for the dough was warmed in a copper. The oven itself has a tile floor, and its door, one jamb for which remains, was set beneath a smoke hood.

The brewhouse lies next to the latrine tower and has two settings for coppers. Water was boiled in the larger copper and poured onto the ground malt. The 'wort' (malted water) was drained off and boiled with hops in the small copper. Fermentation of the wort then took place and the beer was eventually stored in casks. Yeast from the brewing process

Top: This Flemish illustration of about 1440 shows bread rolls being prepared and baked in an oven
Above: The large bread oven in the bakehouse. The small boiling furnace can be seen to the right of the opening
Below right: The settings for the two large coppers in the brewhouse
Below: This Hambleton ware cistern from the 14th or 15th century, found at Helmsley, was used for decanting ale. The hole at the base held a tap

would have been used in the adjacent bakery to raise the bread dough. The date and function of the rectangular building adjacent to the bakehouse is unknown.

▣ NORTH GATE AND NORTH CURTAIN WALL

The northern curtain wall has a twin-towered D-shaped gatehouse, with an inward-opening doorway and portcullis, and circular towers at the extreme corners of the curtain wall. All four towers had rear walls and internal rooms for basic accommodation and storage. Only the lower parts of the towers survive, and it is not possible to estimate how high they were, but they must have had at least a ground floor, or basement, with an upper floor and battlements above that. All the towers are different shapes; the north-east tower has a secondary turret on its outer face, an unusual arrangement, similar to turrets at Barnwell Castle, Northamptonshire. Two postern gates, one on the east side of the gatehouse and the other against the north-west tower, gave access to the edge of the rampart. This side of the castle, as built in about 1200, would have formed an impressive frontage. The gatehouse has been compared to the surviving inner gatehouse at Skipton Castle, North Yorkshire, one of the earliest twin-towered gatehouses in the country.

The date and purpose of the rectangular building between the chapel and the north curtain wall are unknown, but it was perhaps the location of a stable documented at the castle in the 16th century.

Above: The base of the north-west corner tower. The finely dressed masonry of the tower contrasts with the rubble facing of the curtain wall

Below: This round tower at Skipton Castle, now sandwiched between later buildings, formed one half of a twin-towered gatehouse. The towers of the north gatehouse at Helmsley may have looked similar

Above: The curved rubble footings of one of the open-backed towers of the north barbican

15 NORTH BARBICAN

Later in the 13th century, when the south barbican was being built, a small barbican with elongated open-backed towers was also added to the northern front. It may have been built for additional protection or perhaps to create an imposing frontage to the castle when viewed from the north. A drawbridge pit was built, with steps leading to a doorway into the ditch; this pit had to be strengthened by a buttress in the 14th century.

This barbican was not as sophisticated as the southern one, implying that the south entrance was the main point of access by the later 13th century. The public car park visible beyond the castle at this point is on the site of the medieval gardens and orchard, so the north gatehouse and its barbican represented a private area, leading to a landscape used only by the castle's lords and guests.

16 WEST RANGE EXTERIOR

A walk along the outer bank from the north barbican, towards the south-west, provides views not only of the castle's west range, but also of the 18th-century parkland of the Duncombe

Right: The exterior of the west range from the south-west

A Curtain wall

B Latrine tower

C 14th-century windows lighting the latrines

D Window lighting floors added in 16th or 17th century

E Chamber block

F Elizabethan windows

G 12th-century doorway that originally led to a wooden bridge across the inner ditch

H West tower

I Doorway onto chamber block roof

J Blocked 14th-century windows

K West tower basement window

estate beyond the walled garden. This parkland is on the site of the medieval castle's inner park known as Le Haye, and the West or New Park.

The various phases of building and rebuilding of the castle are clear when viewing the western range from the outer bank. The rocky ridge upon which the castle sits is evident from this side; the stone from the ditch provided the grey masonry of the curtain wall. The two small windows in the latrine tower lit the 14th-century latrines; above are the windows of the floors added in the 16th and 17th centuries. The windows of the central block belong to the Manners' mansion, replacing medieval windows. At the south-east end of this range is the west tower, its outer face and buttressing dating from the late 13th or early 14th century. Near the top of the tower a doorway leads onto the roof of the chamber block. In the outer face the windows are Elizabethan, apart from the three central ones, which date from the 14th century. The two upper windows were blocked by fireplaces; the ground-floor example retains its metal fittings. The outfall of the basement drain is visible between two buttresses.

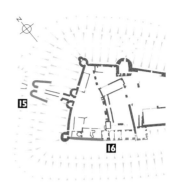

Helmsley Archaeology Store

Helmsley is the location of English Heritage's North of England Archaeology Store. This purpose-built depository houses archival material and over 50,000 objects dating from prehistory to the modern day.

After Helmsley Castle was taken into State guardianship in 1923, work began to clear the site of accumulated soil and debris, and to consolidate the buildings with the aim of opening the site to visitors. The first find, a silver coin dated 1697, was noted as being uncovered in the 'bottom storey' of the west tower on 2 February 1924. In total 162 groups of finds were listed as being found at Helmsley between 1924 to 1931, ranging from quantities of weapons, architectural stone and fittings (such as window glass, frames, door fittings and nails) to ceramic and glass vessels and coins. Small metal finds were sent to the Ministry of Works' headquarters in London for safekeeping, while ceramics and stone remained stored on site. This process was repeated at many guardianship sites throughout the country in the first half of the 20th century, resulting in the accumulation of large numbers of objects.

By the mid 20th century Helmsley Castle had become a central works depot for the Ministry of Works (which later became part of the Department of the Environment and then English Heritage from 1983) serving the maintenance needs of the castle and other local Yorkshire sites. Sheds were built in a works compound on the site of the town gasometer, now the location of the castle's visitor centre. Further work space was rented in a warehouse next to the old railway station. From the late 1980s this warehouse was also used to store finds from other sites in the region, before a

Above: *A silver coin labelled as find number 1 from Helmsley Castle*
Left: *Architectural stonework is stored on industrial racking at Helmsley*

purpose-built modern warehouse, known as the Helmlsey Archaeology Store, was constructed adjacent to it in 1993.

A Varied Collection

Collections from sites across the north of England were then transferred to the Helmsley Store, enabling modern conservation standards to be applied. These include detailed cataloguing and research, repacking, cleaning, and monitoring of temperature and relative humidity to safeguard the collections for future generations. The majority of the space is taken up with architectural stone from castles and abbeys as well as Roman sites, but the store also houses many other types of objects recovered through archaeological investigation and conservation.

The majority of the objects found at Helmsley Castle are on display here, but the store contains further pallet loads of ceramic fragments, roofing slates, architectural stone and 16th-century oak panelling from the west range. As with all sites the objects are catalogued in a national database. These collections often form a significant element of our knowledge about how sites were used in the past.

Architectural stone is studied to reveal information about lost buildings, often informing reconstruction drawings of how sites may have looked. Research is carried out on small finds to identify and date them accurately. Ceramic assemblages are similarly analysed and are good indicators of specific activities, trade networks and when sites were in use.

Fascinating Insights

Analysis of even the most unpromising finds can often give information not available from any other source. For example, at Helmsley over a dozen 'hearth bottoms' were recovered during the site clearances in the 1920s; a hearth bottom is slag that forms in a hearth during the blacksmithing of iron. They were not recognised when they were found, but were probably saved and stored because they resembled broken iron cannonballs. Modern analysis, however, carried out over 80 years after they were excavated, has allowed them to be identified, and they now represent the only evidence of ironworking at the castle.

They had a high iron content and were probably used by a very skilled blacksmith, such as an armourer, to help regulate the temperature of his hearth. Further analysis compared the iron composition with that of the Civil War cannonballs from Helmsley, and determined that the cannonballs were made off-site and were not from a known local smithy.

Access

Helmsley Archaeology Store is open to general visitors on advertised open days and researchers are able to use the facility year-round. Volunteers provide invaluable assistance to staff with the care of this significant collection.

Above: Two 'hearth bottoms' recovered from Helmsley Castle. The lower one has been sectioned to analyse its composition

Left: This large stone from Helmsley Castle, now in store, has been carved with a Nine Men's Morris board, giving an insight into medieval pastimes at the castle

History of the Castle

BEFORE THE CASTLE

The settlement that became the market town of Helmsley lies on the north bank of the river Rye, with direct connections to York and to other towns with major castles, such as Pickering and Scarborough. Very little is known about Helmsley before the castle was built. Evidence of prehistoric activity, including round barrows, can be seen in the surrounding countryside. A small hoard of Roman silver coins deposited in the early third century was found at Helmsley before 1931, and a substantial villa existed at Beadlam, about one mile to the east of Helmsley (the finds from this site, including a mosaic, are in the Helmsley Archaeology Store). Place names in the area attest to both Anglo-Saxon and Viking settlements, and in Helmsley Church there is a 10th-century Anglo-Scandinavian hogback tomb.

At the time of the Domesday survey (1086) the manor of 'Elmeslac' was owned by Count Robert of Mortain (c.1031–90), half-brother to King William I (r.1066–87), but there is no evidence that he built a castle here. There was a church with a priest at that time, but the estate was valued at 10s., as opposed to the 32s. it had been worth in the time of Edward the Confessor (r.1042–66). The drop in value was presumably a result of the 'Harrying of the North' by King William from 1069 to 1070, the brutal suppression of a rebellion that resulted in depopulation and the destruction of land and buildings. According to the Domesday survey there were possibly seven men and their families living on the estate – perhaps about 30 people – and although there was some waste land around the settlement, evidence of William's 'Harrying', there was also woodland, pasture and arable land. The name Helmsley appears in documents throughout the Middle Ages in various guises, such as 'Hamelak' and 'Haumesley'.

Above: Roman silver denarii from a hoard of 34 coins discovered in Helmsley before 1931. The coins were probably hidden about the year AD 218

Left: Scene from the Bayeux Tapestry showing William, Duke of Normandy with his half-brother, Robert of Mortain (labelled 'Rotbert'), sitting to his left. The manor of Helmsley was in Robert's possession at the time of the Domesday survey

Facing page: Watercolour of the east tower by Francis Grose (1731–91) showing the inner bailey overgrown and with a great build-up of soil and debris

Above: A 13th-century portrait of Aelred from a manuscript of his Speculum caritatis, *'The Mirror of Charity'*

WALTER ESPEC AND THE FIRST CASTLE

Count Robert lost his estates as a result of his rebellion in 1088 against King William II (r.1087–1100), and although restored to the family, they were lost again by Robert's son, William, when he rebelled against King Henry I (r.1100–35).

The Mortain lands were granted to Walter Espec in about 1122; Walter also held lands in Northumberland, at Wark on the river Tweed. He was a loyal servant to the Crown, undertaking various duties in the North. When David I, King of Scots (r.1124–53), invaded England, Espec was one of the commanders who defeated him at the Battle of the Standard, near Northallerton, in 1138. In the 1150s Espec is said to have retired to Rievaulx Abbey, which he had founded in 1132, and he may have died in 1154. The castle passed to his brother-in-law, Peter de Ros I, who had married Adelina, Espec's sister. When Peter de Ros died in 1157 he was buried at Rievaulx Abbey and the estate passed to Robert de Ros I (d.1167) and then to his son, Everard (d.1182/3).

Walter Espec and Rievaulx Abbey

Helmsley Castle has always been closely connected with the fortunes of nearby Rievaulx Abbey through its patrons, Walter Espec and the de Ros lords of Helmsley.

The abbey was founded in 1132 by the Cistercian order of monks to establish a base for their order in the north of England. Initially some 23 men (the abbot, 12 monks and 10 lay brothers) came from the monastery of Clairvaux in eastern France, but by the later 1100s, the community had grown to over 600. The lay patron of the abbey was Walter Espec, lord of Helmsley and builder of the first castle there. A supporter of the Cistercians and ecclesiastical reform, he donated the land on which the abbey and its estates were to be built.

Arguably the most famous monk at the abbey was the Northumbrian Aelred (1110–67). He joined the community at Rievaulx in 1134, after staying with Espec at Helmsley Castle for two nights, visiting the abbey and being impressed with what he found there. He became abbot in 1147 at the age of 37, and was later made saint (1250). Aelred was a renowned scholar and administrator and the author of a number of canonical texts.

The first castle was built at Helmsley during Walter Espec's lifetime. There is very little evidence for its form, although a 12th-century sermon by Abbot Aelred of Rievaulx, an associate of Walter Espec, perhaps gives a clue as to its main elements – Rievaulx Abbey stood only three miles from Helmsley, and the castle may have inspired Aelred's description: *'Three things make a castle strong: a moat, a wall, and a tower. First the moat, then the wall rising above the moat, and finally the tower, which is stronger and more significant than the other two.'*

It is clear that the castle stood on the rocky ridge, cut off with earth ramparts and ditches. The ramparts were probably topped by a timber palisade. The outer bailey to the south may have been part of this first castle. The main platform was divided in two by a curtain wall, presumably with a ditch, and the footings of this wall survive, running from under the later west tower towards the 13th-century chapel. Parts of the outer wall of the chamber block may also date from Espec's time, but no other traces of this first castle can be seen.

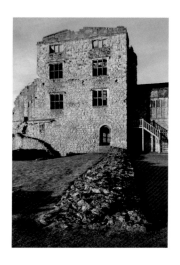

Above: The 2m-wide footings of a wall that divided the inner bailey of Walter Espec's castle can still be seen

Aelred wrote an account of the Battle of the Standard, fought between the English and the Scots in August 1138. His text provides a vivid contemporary description of Walter Espec:

'Also present was Walter Espec, an old man, and full of days, sharp-witted; wise in his advice, restrained in times of peace, farsighted in war, steadfast in his friendship towards allies and in his constant loyalty to kings. He was of immense physical stature, all his limbs of such size that they exceeded the norm; and were in proportion to his great height; his hair was black; his beard abundant; his forehead broad and noble; his eyes large, and sharp-sighted; his face very broad, but well-shaped; his voice like a trumpet, combining the eloquence which came easily to him with a certain grandeur of sound. Moreover he was distinguished physically, but more

so for his Christian piety; of course although he lacked children and heirs, he certainly didn't lack vigorous descendants; of each of his best estates he made Christ his heir: for in a most charming place, Kirkham by name, he founded a monastery regular of clerics, embellishing it with many endowments, and enriching it with estates.'

The de Ros Family

Following the death of Walter Espec, the de Ros family became patrons of Rievaulx Abbey as lords of Helmsley throughout the Middle Ages, as well as of nearby Kirkham Priory further east, which was

also founded by Espec. In the 13th and 14th centuries members of the de Ros family were buried at Rievaulx and Kirkham.

After the Dissolution

The relationship between the abbey and the castle came full circle in the 16th century when the Manners family, who owned Helmsley Castle from 1508, acquired Rievaulx at the Dissolution and were responsible for the destruction of the abbey for profit. In the 18th century, the abbey and the castle were afforded renewed importance as romantic ruins and incorporated into the Picturesque landscape of Duncombe Park.

Far left: The dramatic ruins of Rievaulx Abbey
Left: A carved stone peacock, an emblem of the de Ros family, from Rievaulx Abbey

ROBERT DE ROS II AND THE REBUILDING OF THE CASTLE

Much of the castle that we see today dates from the time of Robert de Ros II (c.1182–1226/7), also known as Fursan, the great-grandson of Espec's brother-in-law.

Robert took possession of Helmsley in 1191 and the 12th-century Cartulary of Rievaulx Abbey, a document containing the primary evidence for the abbey's landholdings, states that he 'raised the castles of Helmislay and of Wark', improving the existing castles there. His estates in England and Normandy made him powerful and rich, and his position was further cemented by his marriage to Isabella, an illegitimate daughter of William the Lion, King of Scots.

Although sometimes out of favour, Robert was generally part of the intimate circle of King John (r.1199–1216), campaigning with him in Ireland in 1210. In the baronial revolt against the king, however, when he was Sheriff of Cumberland, Robert eventually sided with the barons. He was one of the 25 lords chosen to ensure that the king complied with the provisions of Magna Carta (1215) and, according to the chronicler Matthew Paris, successfully held Helmsley against the king during his northern campaign in 1216. Robert was a witness to the third reissue of Magna Carta in 1225. Soon after that, he joined the order of the Knights Templar and, following his death in 1226 or 1227, is said to have been buried in the Temple Church, London; the order benefited from several benefactions made by Robert.

Top: View west towards the inner bailey. The south gate, and east and west towers, were all originally built by Robert de Ros in the early 13th century
Above: The 1225 reissue of Magna Carta, witnessed by Robert de Ros II

The building work undertaken by Robert after 1191 transformed Helmsley, equating it with other royal and baronial castles of the period. During his time, the earth and timber defences of Espec's castle were replaced by a stone curtain wall. The rounded and D-shaped towers we see at Helmsley became common in England from the early years of the 13th century. A square gate tower was built at the south-east corner, and this became the main entrance to the castle. Midway along the east curtain wall a large D-shaped tower was built overlooking the town beyond. The northern approach to the castle, which was a secondary or private entrance, was protected by a twin-towered gatehouse and a curtain wall with rounded towers at each end.

The buildings on the west side of the castle, overlooking one of the medieval parks, were altered in the 16th century, but the curtain wall and parts of the hall belong to Robert's time, as does the west tower, which functioned as his solar or private room adjacent to the chamber block to the north-west. Although he held lands elsewhere, Helmsley Castle was Robert de Ros's main residence, and it is likely that he spent a significant part of each year here.

Above: The construction of a fortified building in stone, illustrated in a 13th-century manuscript. Helmsley's earth and timber defences were replaced in stone from the late 12th century

Knights Templar

The order of the Poor Fellow-Soldiers of Christ and of the Temple of Solomon, known as the Knights Templar, were a military religious order founded formally in 1120. They followed the Rule of St Benedict, and their primary mission was to protect pilgrims travelling in the Holy Land, as well as to defend crusader conquests. The first Templars came to England in 1128 and by the 1140s they had a base in Holborn, London, before moving slightly further to the south where they built their new church, consecrated in 1185. Known as the Temple Church, it has a circular nave, a feature of Templar foundations. The Templars established networks throughout Europe to raise funds and enlist recruits for the order in the Holy Land.

When nearing their deaths, many lords became members of the order, making donations in return for prayers. These included Robert de Ros II and William Marshal, Earl of Pembroke (d.1219), one of the greatest knights of Christendom, whose tomb is in the Temple Church, London.

Below: A detail from a map of Jerusalem of about 1200, showing Templars riding into battle

THIRTEENTH CENTURY

William de Ros I (d.1258) succeeded his father as lord of Helmsley, while his brother, Robert (d.c.1270) held Wark in Northumberland. Before his succession, William, like his father, had supported the baronial revolt against King John. Following the king's death in 1216, Henry III was declared king at the age of nine. Many barons chose to abandon the revolt and support Henry, but some, including William, continued in their support of Prince Louis of France, who had invaded England in 1216 at the request of the rebel barons. William de Ros was taken prisoner at the Battle of Lincoln in May 1217 when the rebels were defeated by William Marshal, Earl of Pembroke, and the royalist army, but was released later that year following the payment of sureties. On his death, William de Ros I was buried by the high altar of Kirkham Priory in North Yorkshire. The de Ros family remained patrons of the priory, founded by Walter Espec, for several generations.

William's son, Robert de Ros III (d.1285), succeeded and married the heiress of the Belvoir estate, Isabel d'Aubigny. In 1265, as Lord Ros of Helmsley, he was summoned to the parliament of Simon de Montfort, leader of the dissident barons in conflict with King Henry III. Robert was also buried at Kirkham.

Helmsley remained the main residence of the de Ros family and work on strengthening the castle continued under William and Robert III, although the majority was probably carried out

in the time of Robert, paid for with the wealth he had gained through his marriage. A drawbridge pit with postern was added to the northern gatehouse entrance, and an outer defence or barbican was built on the outer rampart, consisting of two elongated, open-backed towers. A drawbridge pit was also built in front of the south gate with steps leading down to three posterns, and the impressive south barbican with its twin-towered D-shaped gatehouse was also constructed at this time. In the centre of the castle a rectangular chapel was built, consecrated in 1246.

FOURTEENTH CENTURY

Major improvements continued at the castle during the lives of William de Ros II (d.1316), who fought in King Edward I's Welsh wars of 1277 and 1282, as well as in Scotland, and his son William III (d.1343); both are buried at Kirkham. As the defences needed little or no work following the later 13th-century improvements, the new works focused on enhancing the domestic facilities. Certainly the Scots army seems to have avoided the castle following the English defeat at the nearby Battle of Byland or Scawton Moor in October 1322, which resulted in the flight of King Edward II (r.1307–27) from Rievaulx and the subsequent sacking of the abbey.

Rooms were created against the south barbican, and wing walls were added, running down to the ditch and up to meet the southern corners of the castle. The east tower, in which King Edward III (r.1327–77) may have stayed when he visited Helmsley for about five days in 1334, was heightened and rearranged internally to create four floors. Within the inner bailey a kitchen, a pantry and a buttery were built against the southern curtain wall, serving a new aisled hall. The west, solar, tower was enlarged and new windows and latrines were added. At the north-west end of the early 13th-century chamber block the fine latrine tower was built.

An inquisition that followed the death of William de Ros III in 1343 sheds some light on the castle and its environs, mentioning parks and orchards, as well as naming some of the key members of staff: a parker, a constable and a chaplain.

Above: A 14th-century tomb effigy, probably of William de Ros II, in the Temple Church, London. The family crest of three water bougets (leather bags for carrying water) can be seen on the shield

Below: A new hall, built in the early 14th century, may have been the setting for grand feasts like this, from a Flemish manuscript of about 1340

The inquisition also stated that it would cost at least £6 13s. 4d. per year to maintain the castle and the buildings within it in good condition – a surprisingly small sum for such a large castle, suggesting that, as their primary residence, the de Ros lords kept the castle in good repair.

William de Ros IV, who inherited the estate aged about 13, fought in France at Crécy and against the Scots at Neville's Cross, near Durham, both in 1346. He died in 1352 while on pilgrimage to the Holy Land. His brother, Thomas (d.1384), was buried at Rievaulx, as was Thomas's heir, John (d.1393), who died in Paphos, Cyprus, on the way to the Holy Land; his embalmed body was returned to Yorkshire.

LATE MEDIEVAL CASTLE

Through much of the 15th century, Helmsley remained the
Yorkshire seat of the de Ros family, but Belvoir Castle in
Leicestershire became their main home. William de Ros V
(d.1414), who had inherited Helmsley Castle in 1393, was
Lord Treasurer of England (1403–4), and was buried at
Bottesford, Leicestershire, near Belvoir Castle, as were most of
his successors. John de Ros II and his brother, William, were
killed in France at the Battle of Baugé in 1421, during the
Hundred Years War. Another brother, Thomas II (d.1430),
was succeeded by his son Thomas III, who was only three
years old at the time.

Right: King Edward IV (r.1461–70 and 1471–83) witnesses an execution. In 1464 Thomas de Ros III, one of the leaders of a Lancastrian army of rebels against Yorkist King Edward IV, was captured and executed following defeat at the Battle of Hexham

The Wars of the Roses

Thomas de Ros III came of age in 1446 and shortly afterwards travelled to France to serve in the final years of the Hundred Years War. He returned to England and from 1449 attended parliament. During the Wars of the Roses (1455–85) fought between the houses of York and Lancaster, he sided with the Percy family of Northumberland, supporters of Lancastrian Henry VI (r.1422–61 and 1470–71). After the Yorkist victory at the Battle of Towton (March 1461), Thomas III fled to Scotland with Henry, but remained active militarily in the North. In 1464 he took part in the Battle of Hexham, but, following the Lancastrian defeat, he was captured and executed at Newcastle, and buried at Hexham. There is little evidence for building work at Helmsley Castle during this time, apart from the probable addition of the bakehouse and brewhouse.

Following the execution of Thomas III, the castle came into the hands of the Crown, and in March 1478 it was granted to Richard, Duke of Gloucester, the future King Richard III (r.1483–85). On the accession of Henry VII (r.1485–1509) after Richard's death at the Battle of Bosworth, the Helmsley lands were restored to the de Ros family, to Edmund (d.1508). As he was considered to be 'not of sufficient discretion to guyde himself and his lyvelode [livelihood], nor able to serve his highness after his duties', the estates were overseen by Sir Thomas Lovell, his brother-in-law, following an Act of 1492.

THE TUDOR CASTLE

The castle came into the ownership of the Manners family in 1508 through Edmund's nephew, Sir George Manners of Etal in Northumberland. George died during the siege of Tournai in 1513, and his son, Thomas, inherited Helmsley. Thomas was a member of Henry VIII's (r.1509–47) court, and was made Earl of Rutland in 1525. After Rievaulx Abbey was suppressed in 1538 he bought the site and its estate and began to dismantle the abbey buildings systematically, salvaging any materials of value; the west window of the abbey church was transferred to Helmsley Castle at a cost of £3 13s. 4d.. He died in 1543.

After the death of the second earl, Henry, in 1563, Helmsley passed to the third earl, Edward (1549–87), who resided mainly at Belvoir Castle, Leicestershire. Helmsley was refurbished as a grand country house. The medieval lodgings range was adapted to create new apartments, with fine plasterwork incorporating the coat of arms of the third earl and his wife, Isabel Holcroft, decorating the ceiling and walls of the first-floor rooms. The latrine tower and the west tower were also remodelled, and a new wing was built running across the inner bailey from the lodgings range to the north-east corner, with a long gallery on its upper floor. The gatehouse in the south barbican was also refurbished, with its fine tympanum above the lintel and passageway possibly reusing stone from Rievaulx Abbey.

The building works appear not to have progressed smoothly, however, and a letter of April 1578 from Edward's agent, William Segrave, to the earl states 'Your buildings at the Castle [Helmsley] here do not proceed so speedily as the

Below: Effigy of Thomas Manners, 1st Earl of Rutland, from his tomb in St Mary the Virgin's Church, Bottesford, Leicestershire
Bottom: A 19th-century evocation, in watercolour, by William Richardson, of one of the upper rooms of the chamber block, as it may have appeared following the Manners family's refurbishments

mason supposed. The mason's work will not be ended before Lammas [1 August].' A letter of 1580 from George Lockwood, another agent acting on the earl's behalf, mentions payments of £10 owed to a mason, Peter Urselay, and that the plasterer had completed his work. Lockwood expressed concern that the windows had yet to be glazed and that the plasterwork would be affected by the weather. The building work was probably completed by the late 1580s.

The third earl died in 1587 and Helmsley passed to his brother, John (4th Earl of Rutland, d.1588). Helmsley Castle remained in the possession of the Earls of Rutland throughout the late 16th and early 17th centuries. An inventory of the

Above: *The arms of Edward Manners, 3rd Earl of Rutland, and his wife, Isabel Holcroft in the first floor of the chamber block. The plaster was originally picked out in colour – traces of paint can still be seen*

Facing page top: *Fragments of 17th-century chargers (large serving dishes), found at the castle: an English tin-glazed dish (top); and a more unusual slipware example imported from the Netherlands or the lower Rhine (below). These good-quality wares suggest a high standard of living at Helmsley*

Right: *Reconstruction of the castle in about 1600 following the creation of the Tudor mansion. It is not clear whether the medieval hall was still standing at this time, as shown here*

A Remodelled south
   barbican gatehouse
B Medieval hall
C Heightened west tower
D Chamber block
E Loggia
F Long gallery
G Tudor garden
H Tudor kitchen adapted from
   former chapel
I Heightened latrine tower
J Brewhouse
K Bakehouse

castle from 1636, one of several 17th-century inventories now held at Belvoir Castle, the main seat of the Manners family, mentions many of the functional rooms within the castle at that time, including the hall, the great chamber, the dining room and the lord's bed chamber. It also lists two rooms in the tower, a parlour, a storehouse, a pantry, a cellar, a kitchen and pastry, a kitchen chamber and stables, and a high chamber, although surprisingly, the long gallery appears not to have been listed. It is not clear where some of these rooms might have been located. Many of the items of furniture in these rooms were described as 'old', suggesting that the family did not spend much time at Helmsley.

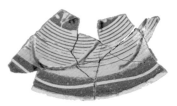

Above: Copy of a 1628 portrait by
Gerrit van Honthorst of George
Villiers, 1st Duke of Buckingham, his
wife, Katherine Manners, and two of
their children, Mary and George (who
became 2nd Duke of Buckingham)
Below: Cannon shot found at
Helmsley Castle. The location of these
finds suggests that, during the Civil
War siege, Parliamentary ordnance
was concentrated on the east tower,
the north-western defences and the
south gate

THE CIVIL WAR AND AFTERMATH

Earl John's sons Roger (d.1612) and Francis (d.1632) became
the 5th and 6th Earls of Rutland. Francis's daughter, Katherine,
married the royal favourite George Villiers, 1st Duke of
Buckingham, in 1620. Katherine had to renounce her
Catholicism in order to marry, but later reverted and became
fervent in her beliefs. An extremely rich woman, Katherine
became a favourite of King Charles I (r.1625–49), who was
also married to a Catholic, and his Court. A contemporary
described her as a woman of 'very great wit and spirit'.
Helmsley eventually passed to their son George, the second
duke (d.1687).

During the civil war between King Charles I and Parliament
that began in 1642, Helmsley was garrisoned by the Royalists
under the command of local man Sir Jordan Crosland who had
been knighted and appointed a Colonel of Horse in 1642.

After the Parliamentary success at the Battle of Marston
Moor in July 1644 and the subsequent fall of the city of
York, the Parliamentary General Thomas Fairfax turned his
attention to Helmsley Castle in late August that year. In the
Parliamentary newspaper *Perfect Occurrences* for the week
ending 6 September, it was reported that 'Our Canon are
planted before Hemsley Castle and we hope speedily to take
it'. Less auspiciously, it was also stated that 'Sir Thomas Fairfax
is most unfortunately shot in the shoulder, by a bullet from
the Enemie in Hemsley Castle.' The circumstances of his
injury are not known for certain: one contemporary
pamphlet asserted that he was wounded while 'viewing
the ground for raising of his Batteries, and planting of
his Ordnance', while another said that the wound was
received while leading his men in an attack.

In early November 1644, Royalist cavalry from Pontefract, Knaresborough and Skipton tried to lift the siege, but were driven off. Although the Royalist paper *Mercurius Aulicus* claimed that they had managed to scatter the besieging force, take prisoners and capture munitions and provisions, Parliament's paper *Perfect Diurnall* reported that the story did not end quite so well for the Royalists: the besiegers regrouped and defeated the relieving force, taking 80 horses and supplies destined for Helmsley, as well as prisoners, listing the names of a captain, six lieutenants, a cornet and an ensign, and 44 other men. Only five Parliamentarians were wounded, including two lieutenants.

With relief unlikely, Crosland negotiated terms for surrender, listing proposals on 6 November 1644. The castle surrendered soon after. Among the generous terms agreed were that Crosland, his officers and men, with all their goods, could leave freely to join the Royalist garrison at Scarborough Castle. The dowager Duchess of Buckingham's goods, and those of her servants, would remain in the town or castle under Fairfax's protection. Carriages would be provided to carry the light field guns, known as drakes, and munitions to Scarborough. Helmsley Castle was to be 'absolutely demolished', neither side garrisoning it, and prisoners on both sides would be released, including Parliament's Lt-Colonel Forbes, taken prisoner during the siege. A list of fatal casualties published in 1647 names four Parliamentary and Royalist common soldiers killed at Helmsley.

Below: Objects from the Civil War siege have been found at Helmsley, including swords **A** *and spurs such as this one* **B**

Thomas Fairfax

Fairfax was one of Parliament's greatest generals and was instrumental in the creation of the New Model Army, being its commander from 1645–50. He recounted an incident at the siege of Helmsley in his memoirs: *'I went to Helmsley to take in the castle there, where I received a dangerous shot in my shoulder, and was brought back to York, all being doubtful of my recovery for some time.'*

Left: 19th-century copy of an engraving of Thomas Fairfax made about 1647–49
Right: Civil War musket shot from Helmsley

SIR THOMAS FAIRFAX *Knight.*
General of the Forces raised by the Parliament.

'…Wedensday the 10th August, they went to Hemsly Parke, 15 miles from Yorke, where they had a warrant from the Duke of Buckingham for a fat bucke, which they hunted, and had very good sport… In this towne thir is a faire castell, but much of itt ruinated, called Hemsley Castell.' From the memoirs of Marmaduke Rawdon, antiquary, 1664

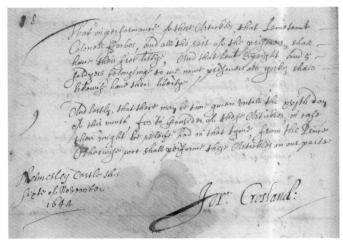

It is clear from the surviving remains that the castle's defences and the east tower were demolished systematically, although this is likely to have taken several years: in 1648 Royalist prisoners taken in the Second Civil War (1648–49) were being held 'in the Dungeon at Helmsley Castle', probably the basement of the west tower.

Fairfax acquired the castle and borough of Helmsley and other properties in 1650. In 1657 his daughter, Mary, married the man from whom Helmsley had been confiscated – the opportunist George Villiers, 2nd Duke of Buckingham – who had gone into exile in 1648 after the Royalist defeat in the Second Civil War, but had returned in 1657. He was imprisoned by Oliver Cromwell in 1658, but was released the following year, his father-in-law financially guaranteeing Buckingham's good behaviour. He regained his properties at the Restoration of Charles II (r.1660–85), and went on to have a political career and a life not free of scandal.

No details are known of how the castle was being used at this time, other than that John Etty of York undertook wainscot work (the creation of wood panelling) at Helmsley for the duke in 1666. The old Tudor mansion continued to be a habitable residence for the duke and his family until his death in 1687.

Top: A document made by Sir Jordan Crosland, 6 November 1644, requesting terms for the surrender of the castle during the Civil War
Above: The antiquary Marmaduke Rawdon, who visited Helmsley in 1664
Right: Portrait of Mary Fairfax, Duchess of Buckingham, after John Michael Wright
Far right: The 2nd Duke of Buckingham by Sir Peter Lely, painted about 1675

Helmsley Town

The building of the castle by Walter Espec and its aggrandisement under Robert de Ros II in the early 13th century led to the growth of the town.

There was a small settlement and a church at Helmsley by the 10th century and by 1210 Robert de Ros II had granted Helmsley borough status – the right to hold markets – and possibly organised the arrangement of houses along Bridge Street, with long, narrow plots behind. The market place was established where it is today by the early 13th century, but it originally occupied the entire area from the parish church to the river Rye, where the lord's mill stood, and westwards towards the castle.

Most of the houses in Helmsley today date from the 17th century onwards. The earliest properties were longhouses, occupied by both families and their livestock. Examples of these (much altered) can still be seen, for example in Bridge Street and Bondgate. Many properties were improved or newly built from the 19th century onwards, often at the instigation of the Duncombe (Feversham) family. A number of inns and hotels were established to cater for tourists and local communities.

The wealth of the area came from agriculture, as well as coal and other natural resources in the surrounding hills. The street name 'Pottergate' on the east side of the medieval town indicates that pottery was made locally, and from the 18th century Helmsley was a small-scale centre for the weaving of linen.

In the late 19th and early 20th centuries, the vicar of Helmsley and the Duncombes were promoters of improvements such as sewer drainage, and the streets were also paved. Domestic gas arrived in 1868, and three years later a railway connection was established. A workhouse, still standing in High Street, was built between 1859 and 1861 to replace a late 18th-century one in Pottergate, and a number of other civic buildings were built in the 19th century.

Above: A monument to William Duncombe, 2nd Baron Feversham (1841–67) stands in the Market Place. The castle's east tower can just be seen behind the buildings
Below: A 1799 engraving of the castle with the town and church beyond

Above: Portrait by John Riley of Charles Duncombe who bought the Helmsley estate in 1695. The poet Alexander Pope later wrote scathingly about the purchase: 'And He[l]msley, once proud Buckingham's delight, Slides to a scrivener, or a city knight'
Below: A fragment from a wine bottle, embossed with the Feversham arms, found at Helmsley Castle
Bottom: The west range and inner ditch by Samuel Bough (1822–78)

EIGHTEENTH AND NINETEENTH CENTURIES

By an Act of 1689 the trustees of the estate were permitted to sell Buckingham's properties, and in 1695 a London banker, Charles Duncombe, purchased Helmsley and its 16,000ha (40,000 acre) estate for the considerable sum of £90,000. On his death in 1711, his brother-in-law and business partner, Thomas Browne, inherited the property, taking the name of Duncombe.

Charles, whose main residence was Downton in Wiltshire, must have occupied Helmsley Castle when visiting the North. Thomas, however, built a new house to a 1713 design by William Wakefield of nearby Huby Hall, seemingly with the advice of the great architect Sir John Vanbrugh. The surrounding landscape was redesigned during the 18th century. From this point onwards, Helmsley Castle was no longer lived in, and gradually fell into ruin.

In the 18th and early 19th centuries artists of the Picturesque movement, in search of wild landscapes and with an appreciation of historic ruins, often stayed in or passed through the town of Helmsley. There are pencil drawings of the castle in the sketchbooks of JMW Turner, but the majority of artists concentrated on depicting Rievaulx Abbey.

Between 1843 and 1847 the architect Sir Charles Barry added wings to Duncombe Park for William Duncombe, Lord Feversham, and further additions and rebuilding were undertaken following the fire of 1879, when the house was gutted, and a smaller fire in 1895.

Various parish events were held in the castle grounds, arranged by the redoubtable Charles Norris Gray, vicar of Helmsley from 1870 until his death. These included fêtes,

historical pageants in 1897 and 1898, parish events, agricultural shows and a tennis tournament. In 1876 the 10th North Riding of Yorkshire Rifle Volunteer Company drilled there.

CASTLE IN THE TWENTIETH CENTURY

Photographs of the castle in the late 19th and early 20th centuries show that little was left of the Tudor house, the latrine tower was roofless, the medieval ruins were covered in ivy, and trees were growing in the ditches and the interior. The Helmsley Tennis Club had its courts in the inner bailey and the level of the interior was much higher than it is today; a ring for tethering horses can be seen at a considerable height on the northern side of the latrine tower.

The castle was taken into State guardianship in 1923, in the care of the Office of Works (English Heritage from 1983). Sir Charles Peers, Chief Inspector of Ancient Monuments, tackled the restoration work over some ten years, with an enthusiasm that would not necessarily meet modern conservation standards. The ruins were consolidated and conserved, the latrine tower was given a new roof, and four timber bridges had been built to provide safe public access by the early 1930s. More drastically, during the economic Depression of the early 1930s, unemployed labourers were engaged to dig and reform

Top left: Children from the Helmsley Wesleyan Day School taking part in a pageant at the castle, 29 April 1900
Top right: Restoration of the oak panelling in the chamber block, 1928
Above: The inner bailey before clearance of the site in the early 20th century. The tennis court can be seen laid out in front of the west range
Below: Glass bottles for 'Atkinson's Aerated Water' found at the castle. These were made in the town and embossed with an image of the castle

Tom Dale (1872–1950)
One of the first custodians at the castle was Tom Dale. His uniform, like that of other custodians, was modelled on those designed for prison warders, and he occupied a hut inside the double gates that look down to Castlegate. He had served with Lord Feversham on the Western Front and his association with the family led to his appointment after the First World War. He worked at Helmsley until 1947.

Below: Helmsley Castle viewed from across Duncombe Park

the ditches and ramparts, in the course of which an original gap at the south-west corner of the outer rampart was filled in. The clearance work revealed large quantities of objects, all of which were recorded in a book, with their dates and locations of discovery. Some of these finds are now on display at the castle and others are kept in the Helmsley Archaeology Store.

It is not known for certain whether the castle earthworks were incorporated into town defences in the Second World War when Duncombe Park's grounds became a military camp, but anti-tank defences still remain in the town, visible as boundary and garden walls.

THE CASTLE TODAY

In 1957 the remains of the brewhouse and bakehouse were cleared, but no dating evidence was found for them. In 1985, when the area to the north of the castle was designated as a new car park, an excavation revealed a leat and other features such as earth banks, which may have been part of medieval gardens and orchards associated with the castle. To the south of the castle, a geophysical survey of the outer bailey in 1995 revealed evidence for structural remains, but no further work was undertaken to interpret them.

Castle studies are a thriving subject, and the authors of recent studies of Helmsley have proposed a number of different theories about aspects of the castle's architecture, such as the dating of improvements to the gatehouse of the south barbican. A systematic analysis of the 17th-century inventories held at Belvoir Castle would enhance our understanding of the layout of the Elizabethan mansion and add another chapter to our knowledge of one of the finest castles of northern England.